How to be a Viking
in 13 easy stages

Contents

Written and illustrated by Scoular Anderson

Collins

STAGE 1 — Call yourself a Viking

You can only call yourself a Viking if you come from the
northern part of Europe called Scandinavia. In Viking times,
there were many tribes living there. The old Viking lands are
now called Sweden, Norway and Denmark.

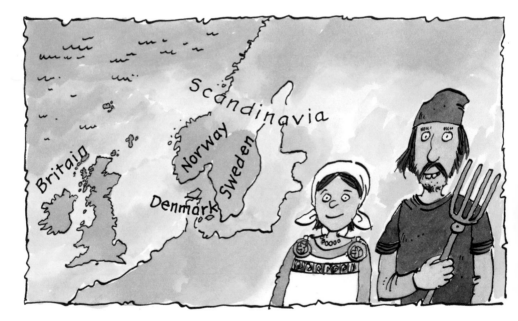

No one is really sure why these people were called Vikings.
Some say the name comes from their word *vik*, meaning a bay,
because the Vikings liked to hide their ships in bays when they
were out raiding.

2

Between the years 793 and 1066 the Vikings often raided Britain, and sometimes brought their families and stayed for good. That's why there are places in Britain with Viking names. We still use quite a few Viking words like window, knife, egg and ski.

Viking words

1 vik - a bay
2 thing - a meeting place
3 by - a farm
4 ness - a headland
5 kirk - a church
6 toft - a house
7 fors - a waterfall
8 thveit - a meadow
9 dale - a valley
10 ay - an island

① Lerwick
⑤ Kirkwall
⑩ Eriskay
⑦ High Force
⑧ Bassenthwaite
Denby Dale ⑨
② Thingwall
③ ④ Grimsby Skegness
③ Derby
Lowestoft ⑥

These words are usually added to other words to make a name. For example: Grimsby means "Grimm's Farm".

STAGE 2

Milk a cow

Most Vikings were farmers. Each farmer and his family lived in a long, single-storey house made of wood, stone or **wattle and daub**. The roof was made of thatch or turf.

fire for cooking in middle of house, with pots hung from beams

wooden chests for storing things

Inside, the farmer, his family and servants lived and slept in one big room. There was a pen at one end, where the animals stayed in winter.

The farmers kept cows, sheep, goats, horses, pigs, chickens and geese. They grew vegetables like onions, leeks, cabbages and peas. They gathered berries, nuts and mushrooms from the woods. In their fields they grew cereals to grind into flour to make bread.

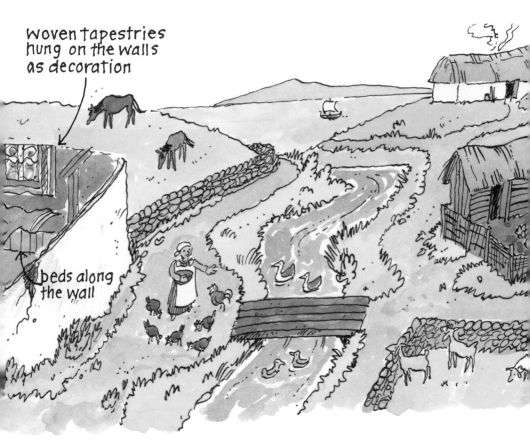

woven tapestries hung on the walls as decoration

beds along the wall

Much of the land in Scandinavia was mountainous and barren. When there was a shortage of good land for farming, the farmers had to go elsewhere to set up home.

Build a ship

The Vikings were skilled shipbuilders. Their warships were called longships. They were long and thin and moved quickly over the sea using a single sail. Oars were used in calm weather and when the ship was close to shore. The longships were light and could sail into shallow water to be pulled up on the beach or even carried overland.

The oarsmen sat on a chest which contained their belongings.

steering oar

oars →

6

If you wanted to transport cargo or
animals you used a knarr.
This ship was broader and
deeper than the longship.

a knarr

supports for
mast when it
was lowered

overlapping
planks called
strakes

rack to hold
shields

holes or ports
for oars

7

Vikings liked to wear colourful clothes that were often decorated with fur, embroidery or metal. The women wore long dresses that were covered by an apron held in place at the shoulders with round clasps. After they were married, women covered their hair with a scarf.

rich women → wore make-up

a chain with useful things like keys, scissors and a sewing kit

Men wore short tunics. There were many styles of
trousers – baggy, tight-fitting, flared or short.
In winter, they wore many layers of clothes with thick
cloaks and fur hats to keep themselves warm.

Both men and women wore their hair long. They liked
to braid their hair and even their beards into pigtails.

Enjoy yourself

STAGE 5

The Vikings weren't always farming or sailing their ships.
Now and then they had some free time. During dark
winter nights they danced and sang round the fire.
They played music on harps and pipes made of bone.

They enjoyed board games like chess and a similar game called
hneftafl. Children played with toys carved out of wood.

In the summer they liked to go on picnics and took part in all sorts of competitions.

In their wrestling matches, the wrestler who forced his opponent onto a stone in the middle of the pitch was the winner.

They liked to place bets on rowing and horse races.

They showed off their strength and skill at fencing, archery and throwing heavy stones.

11

Make something

Viking women made most of the clothes for their families. They wove the cloth on a tall loom which leant against the wall of the house. At the bottom of the loom, the threads were tied round stones to keep them tight. At the top, the finished cloth was wound round a pole.

Thread for weaving was made from sheep's wool or from a plant called flax which they grew in their fields.

spinning wool into thread ↓

← Flax had to be soaked and beaten to get fibres for making thread.

12

The Vikings liked to decorate things with patterns and pictures. They were skilled at carving wood and making beautiful metal objects.

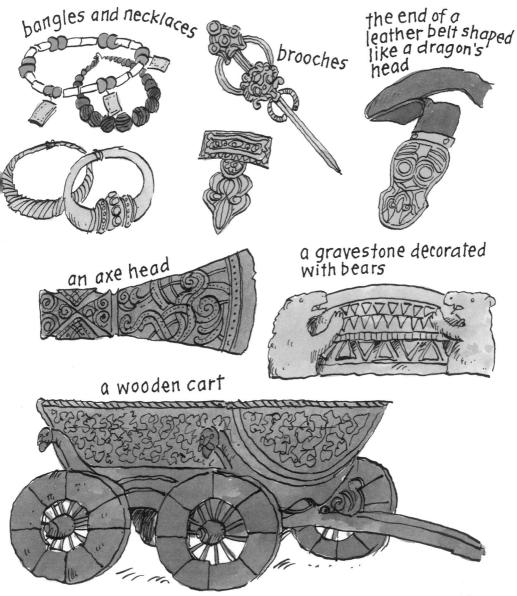

bangles and necklaces

brooches

the end of a leather belt shaped like a dragon's head

an axe head

a gravestone decorated with bears

a wooden cart

Choose a sword

The Vikings' favourite weapons were swords and battle-axes. One of the busiest Vikings was the **metalsmith**. There were always metal objects to be mended and weapons to be made. Swords were made by twisting and flattening strands of metal together which made them flexible, yet strong.

Sword handles were usually decorated with patterns. A good sword was very valuable. It was often given a name and handed down from father to son.

some Viking sword names:

Adder   Fierce
Leg-biter   Mail-biter
Golden-hilt   Long-and-sharp

This groove made the blade more flexible.

In battle, the Vikings wore chainmail to protect their bodies.
Their helmets often had nose and eye guards.

chainmail
coat

wooden
shield
with metal
rim

Some Vikings were known as **Berserkers**.
They used to work themselves up for battle by
shouting insults, throwing stones and biting
the edges of their shields. If someone throws
a noisy tantrum today we might say that they
are going berserk.

Worship gods

The Vikings worshipped many gods. They often threw valuable items like swords and jewellery into rivers because they thought this would bring good luck from the gods. When warriors died in battle the Vikings believed they were taken to live with the gods in heaven – a place they called Valhalla.

The Vikings believed the universe had three levels held together by a giant tree called Yggdrasil

Level 1
Asgard and Valhalla, home of the gods

Evil giants, dwarves and sea serpents lived beyond the sea in Midgard.

Level 2
Midgard, home of humans

Level 3
Niflheim-land of darkness, fire and ice

The evil dragon Nidhogg lived in Niflheim.

16

Odin was king of the gods. His two pet ravens Hugin and Mugin were his spies.

Thor was the god of strength, fighting and storms. He created thunder with his hammer.

Frey was the god of rain, sun, fields and forests. He rode a chariot pulled by a wild boar.

Freya was the goddess of love and death. She could change herself into different shapes.

The Valkyries were a band of women warriors, servants of Odin.

The Vikings liked to wear a lucky charm in the shape of Thor's hammer round their necks.

17

Go exploring

The Vikings were very adventurous people and liked to get around. In spring, they lowered themselves down the sides of high cliffs so they could gather seabirds' eggs.

In winter, they used skis and sledges to travel on snow. They made skates out of horse bone and pushed themselves along the ice with a pole.

Above all, they liked to explore the world and travelled great distances in their ships.

They sailed across the Atlantic Ocean and built farms on Iceland. A Viking called Erik the Red sailed further and landed at a place he named Greenland. His son, Lief Eriksson, went even further and explored part of the land we now call Canada.

The Vikings had no maps. They used the facts they knew about the sea to guide them - like the positions of the sun, moon and stars or weather conditions or catching sight of birds, fish, floating wood or seaweed.

STAGE 10

Go raiding

The Vikings went on raids to other lands because they could steal valuable things like weapons, food, cattle and horses. They even took people to use as slaves. Christian churches and monasteries were popular targets because they often had objects made of gold, silver and precious stones.

At first, the Viking raids were quick and violent. They liked to make surprise attacks on their victims then sail away again before the alarm could be raised.

But after a while, instead of sailing away after an attack, the Vikings settled down and stayed. The British Isles was a popular place to raid and stay because the land was good for farming.

where the Vikings settled in Britain

Shetland

Orkney

Outer Hebrides

Inner Hebrides

Scotland

This part of England was called the Danelaw because so many Vikings came from Denmark to live there.

Ireland

Isle of Man

Wales

England

Go trading

Not all the Vikings were violent raiders. They were also well known as merchants who travelled great distances to trade. The Vikings set up their stalls in towns and villages to sell fur, animal skins, rope, timber, feathers for stuffing pillows and walrus tusks for carving.

Goods were paid for with coins or bits of silver cut from jewellery or plates. The correct amount of silver was weighed out on a pair of scales. The scales were collapsable and could be folded away into a little box.

22

In their search for trade, the Vikings travelled as far south as Spain and into the Mediterranean Sea. They returned home with luxury goods like wine, salt, spices, silk and jewels.

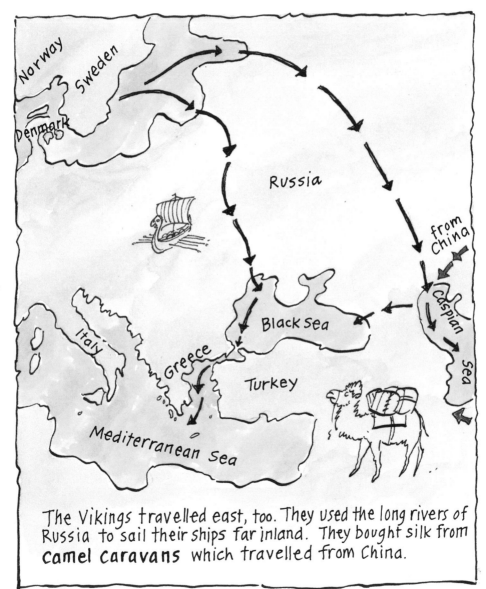

Norway
Sweden
Denmark
Russia
from China
Italy
Black Sea
Caspian Sea
Greece
Turkey
Mediterranean Sea

The Vikings travelled east, too. They used the long rivers of Russia to sail their ships far inland. They bought silk from **camel caravans** which travelled from China.

STAGE 12

Hold a meeting

Most of the Vikings lived on farms or in villages and small towns scattered about the countryside, so once or twice a year they came together at a great meeting. The meeting was called the Thing and was always held in the same place.

At the Thing, relatives and old friends had a chance to meet up with each other. They held a market and kitchens were set up to prepare food for feasts. The Thing was a good excuse to dance, sing, hold sports competitions and catch up on gossip.

The Thing had a serious side too. It was a sort of parliament where important matters could be discussed and decisions made.

The Thing was also a court of law. If someone had committed a crime, the chieftains would decide what punishment was due. This could be anything from a small fine to being hanged, made a slave or banished from the neighbourhood.

Sometimes people took the law into their own hands. If someone felt he or his family had been insulted, it could lead to a fight. These feuds could last for years.

Leave some clues

We know a lot about Vikings because of the clues they left behind. They wrote things down by using marks called runes and carved messages on sticks to send to other people. Here are some letters:

They liked to tell long stories known as sagas. These were exciting tales of adventurous journeys, famous battles and important people. We can read these stories today because they were written down by monks. They give us information about Viking life.

26

When Vikings died, they were usually buried with some of their possessions. A poor person or a slave might be buried with only a knife or a cup. A woman might be buried with part of her weaving loom. A merchant might have his scales or some silver. An important chieftain or his wife was often placed in a ship along with weapons, furniture or jewellery; then the whole ship was buried or burned.

Archaeologists often dig up Viking objects, including whole ships, which help us to understand more about Viking life.

Glossary

Berserkers Viking warriors who worked themselves up for battle by shouting insults, throwing stones and biting their shields. It's said they wore bearskin jerkins called bear sarks and this could be where they got their name from.

camel caravans camels roped together into "camel trains" and used by merchants from the East to carry goods to markets over long distances

hneftafl a board game played by Vikings. It's older than chess. As in chess, players have to plan ahead to outwit each other. Its name means "the king's board" or "the king's game".

metalsmith someone who makes things out of metal

wattle and daub a framework of twigs plastered with clay, straw and dung, used to build houses

Index

The Viking Times

Do you yearn to see the world?
Join Liggi Longnose on his latest voyage of discovery!

Ship leaves for Iceland from North Quay - Thursday.

Siggi's Swords

Swords made to measure
* excellent quality
* fine handling and balance
* high quality decoration

Findra's Fabrics

Top grade cloth for all your dress-making.
Stall 7 Lowthwaite Market

For sale:

lovely home at Bogness close to harbour. House sleeps 20. Big Fireplace. Roomy animal pen. Roof thatch renewed last month.

Hedda's Hairdressing Salon

Have your beard plaited in latest style for your next raid!

reasonable prices

Come and meet at the
Thing
— High Fors —
last full moon of August

* Meet old friends and relatives.
* Enjoy the party atmosphere.
* Get your complaints off your chest.
* Shop till you drop!

See you there!

Thing Rock

High Fors

Coming soon... to a fireside near you...

Eldgrim's Saga

Hear
* how Bolli beat Gizur at the great wrestling match
* how Gudrun poisoned the Dragon of Orm with her potions

31

🐾 Ideas for reading 🐾

Written by Clare Dowdall PhD
Lecturer and Primary Literacy Consultant

Learning objectives: locate information using a range of features; read information passages and identify the main points by noting and listing key points; infer the meaning of unknown words from the context; present information including relevant details

Curriculum links: History: A Viking case study

Interest words: Scandinavia, raiding, barren, embroidery, braid, opponent, metalsmith, flexible, berserkers, parliament, banished, runes, sagas, archaeologists, infer, index, glossary,

Resources: whiteboard, computer

Getting started

This book can be read over two or more guided reading sessions.

- As a group, create a spider diagram showing what the children know about Vikings before reading.

- Look at the picture of the Viking on the front cover. Help the children to infer information based on the picture, (e.g. *they battled, they decorated their clothing*).

- Using the spider diagram and cover, encourage children to raise questions that the book may answer, e.g. *Who were the Vikings?* List the questions on a whiteboard.

- Read the blurb together and discuss what sort of contents this 'information' book may contain. Establish that it is non-fiction. Ask them where else they may find information about Vikings.

Reading and responding

- Read the contents through together and ask children to infer features of Viking life, (e.g. *they were farmers*) Add these ideas to the spider diagram.

- Explain that they are going to find information to answer the question: *Who were the Vikings?* Model how to find this information from the contents, text and pictures, using skimming and scanning as necessary.